Upa

"As one whose own work with Roman Catholic apologists has benefitted tremendously from Eric Svendsen's, I eagerly looked forward to this book from the moment I heard of its inception. With a delightful wit, obvious reversals, and simple applications of logic all informed by extensive experience with Roman Catholic apologists, Svendsen demonstrates conclusively that the most popular and entrenched arguments of those apologists fail to meet their own criteria of truth and verifiability. Svendsen enables average Protestant laymen—especially those who have no formal apologetic or theological training—to understand the crucial issues clearly. Particularly helpful are the analyses of the flawed comparison of Roman 'unity' to Protestant 'anarchy' (Chapter 2) and the fallacious nature of the common '25,000 denominations' argument (Chapter 9).

"This book is a must-read for anyone wishing to have a solid foundation from which to engage in the double responsibility of casting down Roman Catholic imaginations that exalt themselves against the knowledge of God and building a positive case for God's ongoing work of reforming His Church in our day and beyond."

—Tim Enloe, Grace Unknown Online
http://www.graceunknown.com

"I know from personal experience that the Catholic arguments refuted in this book are popular. They're used to some extent by at least the large majority of Catholic apologists. Some of the arguments are found in the allegedly infallible teachings of the Catholic hierarchy. What are we to think of a belief system that misrepresents issues as foundational as the ones discussed in this book? Catholics don't need to clean their house. They need to abandon it. The errors are that significant. This book not only shows that Catholics are wrong in some of the earliest steps of their logic, but also opens the door to discussion of the later steps. Once a Catholic acknowledges that we're all on equal ground in evaluating the evidence with our own judgment, that evidence can be shown to be inconsistent with the claims of the Roman Catholic hierarchy."

—Jason Engwer, Christian Liberty web site
http://www.members.aol.com/jasonte

Upon This ^SLIPPERY Rock

Countering
Roman Catholic
Claims to Authority

Eric D. Svendsen

2002 · Calvary Press, Amityville, New York

CALVARY PRESS PUBLISHING
Post Office Box 805
Amityville, NY 11701
1-800-789-8175
www.calvarypress.com

Book design and typography by Studio E Books
Santa Barbara, CA www.studio-e-books.com

Svendsen, Eric D., 1960–
   Upon this slippery rock : countering Roman Catholic claims to authority /
by Eric D. Svendsen.
   ISBN 1–879737–47–7
Suggested subject headings:
      1. Christianity—doctrines.
      2. Religion
      I. Title

10 9 8 7 6 5 4 3 2 1

*To the new breed of Evangelical
"e-pologists" who contend for
the faith over the Internet—
the new battleground
of apologetics.*

Contents

Preface

THIS BOOK is written by a lay-apologist, to lay-apologists, for lay-apologists. The New Testament extols the virtue of the believer who can give a ready defense of the truth (1 Pet 3:15). When Apollos arrived in Achaia he was a "great help" to the church there, "for he vigorously refuted the Jews in public debate, proving from the Scriptures that Jesus was the Christ" (Acts 18:28). We are told many times in the New Testament to hold in high esteem those who have devoted themselves to the ministry of the gospel, "because of their work" (1 Thess 5:12–13; 1 Cor 16:15–16). In other words, the degree to which a Christian is to be honored by the church is (biblically speaking) directly linked to the degree to which that person has committed himself to the work of the gospel.

Unfortunately, in today's professional-ministry oriented, celebrity-minded church, those who receive the most honor are not always those who work the hardest for the truth. I don't wish to paint with too broad a brush here. There are many exceptionally gifted teachers in the church today that have attained celebrity status. That is as it should be. They are being honored the way the Bible tells us to honor such men. Yet, all too typically this is not the kind of person the church at large normally honors. Instead, celebrity status is given to Christian rock performers, and to those who have thought of the most "creative" strategies to "market" the gospel and the church—buzz words that usually imply a watering down of the gospel of Christ. Unfortunately, I know too many men in leadership positions in the church today who are not even biblically astute enough to articulate their faith to the occasional lay-cultist who happens to knock on their door, but are forced by their ineptitude to say "not interested" and to close the door on an opportunity to point out that cultist's error. Yet they are nevertheless somehow regarded as leaders in the church. Conversely, those who work the hardest in defense of the gospel often not only go unrecognized in the church, but are treated with disdain by the former class of uninformed Christians who see little relevance in defending the truth in today's society.

That situation is regrettable. We as a church should seek to honor and esteem what God honors and esteems. That is why I consider it my great privilege to honor and esteem such men and women as these, who lay it all on the line in defense of the truth and let the chips fall where they may; who bear the shame and disgrace that accompanies the cross of Christ—not only by outsiders, but often by other Christians as well. That is the lot of the lay-apologist, who gladly and without complaining tirelessly holds out the Word of truth, in the face of great opposition, to a crooked and perverse generation, enduring the abuse and scorn that accompanies their thankless—yet eternally invaluable—efforts, and asking for nothing in return.

It is in that spirit that I have sought endorsements for this book, not from the usual candidates (the professional class), but from these lay-apologists. I think it is far more valuable (at least for this book) to secure endorsements from those who have real-world experience battling it out on the "front lines" of Roman Catholic/ Evangelical debate, than from those who observe the battle from the ivory tower. After all, who better to endorse the value of this book as an apologetic tool than those who have successfully used its arguments and principles in real-life scenarios?

The reader should not conclude that this action constitutes an admission on my part that I was somehow unable to secure the endorsements of the professional class. On the contrary; anyone who has read my previous volume (*Who Is My Mother?* Calvary Press, 2001) knows that there is no shortage of scholars, theologians, church historians, pastors and the like who are more than willing to endorse my work. Nor should the reader conclude that I have sought the opinion of just anyone from the ranks of lay-apologetics to commend this work. Far from it. Those from whom I have solicited a commendation are those whom I consider to be among the best and the brightest on the Roman Catholic/Evangelical debate scene today. They have shown by their competent and sober handling of the truth in general—and of the issues this book deals with specifically—that their opinions are worthy to be sought. I am profoundly interested in promoting these men, because I believe it is incumbent upon those of us who have a voice in this arena to take every opportunity available to set a biblical precedent for the rest of the church. Recognizing and honoring men such as these, even if no one else follows that precedent, is one way of doing this. It is to men such as these that I dedicate this book.

To our Lord Jesus Christ alone be the glory.

—Eric D. Svendsen

Upon This SLIPPERY Rock

Introduction

THE WORD "epistemology" (ē-pis´-tĕ-mä'-lĕ-jē) comes from the Greek word ἐπίσταμαι (*epistamai*), which literally means "to understand" or "to know." It is the study of the nature and grounds of knowledge itself. It asks the question, "How do you *know* what you know?"

Any statement of knowledge is subject to epistemological inquiry. Let's take an example from a simple childhood song:

> Jesus loves me; this I know.

Epistemology asks: "How do you *know* Jesus loves you?" To which the song would answer:

> Jesus loves me, this I know,
> for the *Bible* tells me so.

Along comes the Roman Catholic apologist: "Ah, but how do you know the Bible really *means* that? Some Protestants believe that Jesus loves everyone, but others (of the Calvinistic variety) believe that Jesus loves only the elect. Both camps insist that theirs is the correct teaching of the Bible. So how do you determine who is right? We Catholics have an infallible interpreter to tell us the true meaning of the Bible:

> Jesus loves me, this I know,
> for the *Roman Catholic Magisterium* tells me so.

15

The typical Roman Catholic line of argument against Protestantism is to ask epistemological (or "how do you know?") questions:

"How do you know, apart from your own fallible private judgment, that what you believe is the truth?"

"How do you know that the denomination you picked is the 'right' denomination?"

"How do you know which books should and should not have been included in the canon of Scripture?"

The intent of such questions is to show the need for an infallible interpreter, so that the Roman Catholic apologist can then present to you Rome's infallible interpreter, and, along with it, Rome's authority. Having been presented with these "how do you know?" questions by many Roman Catholic apologists over the years, I have had ample opportunity to examine them in a great deal of depth. What strikes me most about these questions is the glaring double standard they present for the Roman Catholic apologist. The Roman Catholic apologist poses these questions as though he has somehow escaped the dilemma he thinks he has created for the Evangelical. On the contrary, in formulating his own position on these issues the Roman Catholic apologist must necessarily engage in epistemological fallacies of the most fundamental nature. What follows in the subsequent chapters of this book is a "fleshing out" of those epistemological fallacies.

Just a brief comment about the format this book has taken: Hands down, this has to be the most unique book I've ever written, at least in terms of its format and writing style. As you might expect, epistemology is not one of the lightest subjects in the world to address. I wanted to create a book that is both exhaustive and readable; one that covers the issue completely but doesn't lose its readers in the process. But I also wanted to create a handbook that is practical in its ability to equip the layman with useful information when confronting the claims of modern Roman Catholic apologists. In order to accomplish this I had to exercise a bit of creativity in the way I presented the concepts.

The reader will find a mixture of literary styles employed throughout this small book; from prose to didactic to humor. I have created real-life scenarios that the reader may very well encounter in his dealings with Roman Catholic apologists (if he has not encountered them already), to give him an idea of what to expect from the Roman Catholic apologist, as well as how best to answer him. These scenarios are followed by a further explanation of why that particular Roman Catholic argument is faulty, and further ways to address that argument. It is hoped that this format will help draw the reader in, and aid him in assimilating these all-important concepts. It is further hoped that this book will equip its readers to recognize the underlying fallacies behind the arguments for Roman Catholic authority; and in turn to help lead their Roman Catholic friends to the true Gospel of Jesus Christ, and to the true source of apostolic faith—*sola Scriptura*.

1. Roman Blitzkrieg

MARK STARED at his computer screen, the questions still echoing in his mind. Questions he had never been asked before. Questions he had never considered. *Questions he didn't know how to answer.* Just moments ago he had for the first time in his life stumbled upon a Catholic-operated Internet chat room. Being an Evangelical Christian, and normally disinterested in anything Roman Catholic, Mark had decided quickly to move on to something of a more Christian nature. After all, it didn't take a genius to figure out that the Roman Catholic church doesn't follow the Bible—in Mark's view, the *final* authority. Mark had raised his mouse pointer to the Close option, but was deterred by an instant message from someone with a screen name of *CathoConvert*: "Welcome to CathoChat! I'm your chat-room host."

Wanting to be polite, Mark responded briefly and clicked the Reply button: "Thanks for the welcome, but I think I'm in the wrong room."

"Oh wait!" the faceless messenger responded immediately, "Are you a Protestant?"

Again driven by civility, Mark responded but was even briefer this time, "Yes."

Mark clicked the Reply button and once again raised his mouse pointer to the Close option. But the odd response that he saw on his computer screen caught his eye and he immediately paused.

"Why?" the message responded.

Rarely had a single word engendered so much puzzlement in him. Curious, Mark decided to stick around just long enough to educate this poor pathetic Catholic who was so obviously unaware of the great disparity between his religion and the Word of God: "Why? Because I believe the Bible, that's why. And because Roman Catholicism contradicts the Bible at so many points, that's why," Mark responded, certain that he had now heard the last of his Catholic inquisitor.

Within seconds, however, another message appeared.

"But how can you be certain that *your* interpretation of the Bible is correct? After all, the Catholic belief has been the constant belief of the Church founded by Jesus Christ for 2,000 years. What makes you think your *private* interpretation should overrule the Church's 2,000-year teaching pedigree?"

With a bit of frustration, Mark responded.

"But this *isn't* just my private interpretation; it is a view that is shared by many Evangelical Protestants."

Barely enough time to catch his breath, Mark's shoulders slumped as he watched yet another response from the faceless messenger flash across his screen.

"Yes, and to which one of the 25,000 Protestant denominations do you belong?"

"Twenty-five *thousand* Protestant denominations? There can't possibly be that many," Mark thought to himself. Then he responded: "Well, I attend a non-denominational Evangelical church."

"Oh, I see," replied the faceless messenger, "That means you disagree with other 'Bible only' Christians, such as Presbyterians, Lutherans, and others, on the issue of infant baptism. And of course you differ with other Protestant denominations on issues of Sabbath-keeping, Millennialism, Tribulationalism, and the Spiritual vs. Figurative Presence of Christ in the Eucharist. All of these churches affirm *sola Scriptura*, and claim to derive their beliefs from the Bible alone. Yet they've all come to different conclusions on these issues. How can you be absolutely certain that it is *your* church that is right on these issues and not some other church?"

Mark stared at his computer screen in disbelief. He had always prided himself on his ability to come up with quick answers to on-the-fly Bible questions. But this time he had no response. The fact of the matter was, he *didn't* know how he could be certain he was

right on all these issues while everyone else was wrong. Yet, some-
what oddly, every instinct in him, every fiber of his being screamed
that there was something very wrong with the faceless messenger's
rationale; something very wrong indeed—though just *what* he could
not say. Answer-less for now, and still stunned by the questions,
Mark decided to retreat. He clicked the Close option and shut
down. He had lost the battle; he had now to prepare for the war.

2. Fair Comparisons?

IT WOULD come as no surprise to this author to learn that many who are reading this book may actually have encountered the foregoing scenario before in one forum or another. You are discussing issues of authority with a Roman Catholic friend, when suddenly you are blind-sighted by the infamous "25,000 Protestant denominations" argument. In arguing this way, your Roman Catholic friend hopes to impale you on the horns of a dilemma; namely, you must either accept the authority of the Roman church, or risk having chosen the wrong church out of the 25,000 options available to you today. What your friend has failed to mention—or, more likely, doesn't understand—is that he himself is caught on the horns of that very same dilemma; only to a much greater degree.

In the Fall of 1999 I posted a challenge on my web site to any Roman Catholic who could pin down the official Roman Catholic teaching about certain issues. The challenge was issued in response to the oft-argued line of reasoning that Protestantism is illegitimate by virtue of the differences in belief among 25,000 Protestant denominations—or, as Roman Catholic apologist Scott Hahn and others like to call it, the "anarchy" of Protestantism. Obviously if this line of argument is legitimate, then it must also act as a standard by which to measure the legitimacy of *any* religious system, not just Protestantism. So, I set out to test the Roman Catholic's own system using this same measure.

Surely, anyone who argues so vehemently against the legitimacy of Protestantism by pointing out variations of belief among Protestant denominations would first want to ensure that his own system was not also excluded on those same grounds. It is important to note that the argument is not one of *degree* of difference—it is that there *are* differences, period. One cannot, for instance, argue that his religious system is more legitimate on the basis that there is less disagreement within it than within other systems of belief. It is an all-or-nothing proposition. Either disagreements nullify the legitimacy of a religious system, or they do not. Otherwise, the best that one can argue is that his religious system more nearly conforms to a set standard of unity, but does not actually meet that standard. It is also important to keep in mind that the "diversity of belief" argument is one that was invented by Roman Catholic apologists. We as Evangelicals do not agree with its premise. But any system that argues for an arbitrary criterion for being the "true" church must itself conform to that criterion.

The challenge questions that I posed were of two types. The majority of the questions had to do with the "official" Roman Catholic belief on various doctrinal issues, such as the Inspiration of Scripture, Predestination, the Literal vs. Mythical interpretation of the creation account in Genesis, the validity of the New Mass, and other such Roman Catholic beliefs; all of which are hotly debated issues within the Roman Catholic camp today. The reason I wanted to know what the Roman Catholic position is on these issues is because no one who views Protestantism as illegitimate based on differences of opinion regarding the meaning of the Bible's teaching on certain issues can at the same time be involved in a religious system that itself produces differences of opinion among its adherents regarding its *own* doctrinal issues.

One example of a doctrinal difference within Roman Catholicism that I have found to be extremely effective when debating Roman Catholic apologists is the issue of the Inspiration of the Scriptures. Representing the conservative camp of Roman Catholicism, most Roman Catholic apologists today believe in the full inspiration and full inerrancy of the Scriptures. However, most Roman Catholic scholars today (representing the moderate camp of Roman Catholicism) believe that the Scriptures are inspired only when speaking of matters of salvation. Both camps derive their views from the very same Vatican II document, *Dei Verbum*. The relevant passage reads as follows:

Since therefore all that the inspired authors or sacred writers affirm should be regarded as affirmed by the Holy Spirit, we must acknowledge that the books of Scripture firmly,
faithfully, and without error teach that truth which God, for
the sake of our salvation, wished to see confined to the
Sacred Scriptures.[1]

This very same passage is used both by Roman Catholic apologists
to support their view that the Bible is fully inspired and inerrant,
and by Roman Catholic scholars to support their view that the
Scriptures are *not* fully inerrant. The former interprets this document as teaching that *all* Scripture is without error, whereas the latter points to the phrase "for the sake of our salvation" as the
modifier to inerrancy. According to the latter view only those passages of Scripture that address specific matters of salvation are to be
considered inerrant. Consequently, and in spite of the Roman Catholic apologist's claims to the contrary, no one can tell us what the
"official" Roman Catholic teaching is on this issue, and Rome's
"infallible interpreter" is of absolutely no advantage to the Roman
Catholic apologist, for he has remained silent in this matter. In order
to arrive at their view of what Rome truly teaches on this issue,
Roman Catholic apologists find themselves in a strange irony. They
must engage in the very same private interpretation in regard to
Roman documents for which they condemn Protestants in regard to
the Bible. In other words, there is just as much diversity of opinion
among Roman Catholics regarding the *meaning* of Roman Catholic
teaching as there is among Protestants regarding the meaning of the
Bible. This confusion is by no means confined to the inerrancy of
Scripture, but is true of many other issues as well. Anyone interested in a fuller discussion of these is referred elsewhere.[2]

When issuing the "25,000 Protestant denominations" argument,
the Roman Catholic is engaging in a false comparison. He would
like to compare the official teaching of Roman Catholicism with the
official teaching of Protestantism. Usually this takes the form
of comparing the Catechism of the Catholic Church (CCC) to
the diversity of beliefs among 25,000 Protestant denominations.

Unfortunately, in doing so the Roman Catholic misses the mark completely because he is comparing the Roman Catholic *rule of faith* to the *various interpretations* of the Protestant *rule of faith*. Let me explain.

The Roman Catholic points to the teaching of the Catechism of the Catholic Church as that which all Roman Catholics must believe to be in communion with Rome—that is, it acts as the Roman Catholic *rule of faith*. Yet the conservative Roman Catholic and the moderate Roman Catholic can read the very same CCC and will invariably arrive at a completely different understanding of what that rule of faith actually teaches. We saw this earlier in our discussion about the inerrancy of Scripture. There we found that both the conservative Roman Catholic and the moderate Roman Catholic can read the same Vatican II document, *Dei Verbum* (which is Rome's "official" statement on this issue), and still disagree about whether or not Rome believes the Bible contains errors.

Now this is precisely the criticism that the Roman Catholic has leveled against the Evangelical principle of *sola Scriptura*. When we as Evangelicals say that the Bible is our *rule of faith*, the Roman Catholic is quick to point out that the Bible is insufficient since there are so many interpretations of it. Yet there are just as many interpretations of the Roman Catholic's own rule of faith as there are of the Bible. The false comparison in which the Roman Catholic engages in such an argument is that he is comparing his rule of faith (viz., the "official" teaching of the Roman Catholic church, usually found in the CCC) to the various *interpretations* of the Evangelical rule of faith, rather than to the Evangelical rule of faith itself (viz., the Bible).

Evangelicals have only *one* rule of faith—the Bible—and that rule of faith remains constant. Of course, as with any document, that rule of faith must be interpreted. Yet, in spite of the insistence of Roman Catholics to the contrary, this does not place Evangelicals at a disadvantage; for the Roman Catholic rule of faith itself (viz., the decrees of popes, councils and the like, culminating in the Catechism of the Catholic Church), being a *document*, must also be interpreted—and it is beyond question that there are various interpretations of that document within the Roman Catholic community. When a true comparison is made, either between the Roman Catholic rule of faith (viz., the CCC) and the Evangelical rule of faith (viz., the Bible)—or between the *various interpretations* of the former rule of faith and the *various interpretations* of the latter rule of faith—it becomes painfully evident that the Roman Catholic "25,000 Protestant denominations" argument is nothing more than an ill-conceived, poorly thought out line of reasoning that is just as devastating to the Roman Catholic position as the Roman Catholic imagines it to be against Evangelicalism.

3. A Romecoming

JUAN SCOTT exited the doors of the church building, feeling a mixture of elation and relief. As he glanced back at the tall, stony architecture, his eyes gazed once more upon the beautiful stained-glass image he had once despised. How odd, he thought, that such a beautiful thing could ever have been the object of his hatred. Silently, he thanked the bearer of the image, his new Blessed Mother, for her seemingly unlimited patience in the face of his unswerving arrogance. But all that was behind him. Today was a new day. A day for which he had been waiting what seemed an eternity to him. A day of new beginnings. It was *the* day. Easter Sunday! Today he had been received back into the One Holy Catholic and Apostolic Church!

The cab he had called had not yet arrived. The bench in front of him beckoned him to sit while he waited, but he was far too energized for that. Received *back*. It all still seemed like a dream to him. He shook his head and smiled at how hardheaded—more, *hardhearted!*—he had been all those years. When he had left the Catholic Church as a young adult, he had done so for all the wrong reasons. Yes, there was corruption in the Church. Yes, she had a checkered past. Yes, the Mass had seemed to be little more than an empty ritual to him. But none of these were valid reasons to leave her. After all, none of these had any bearing on the Church's authority and infallibility. He knew that now. And, he now *understood* the Mass.

As a Protestant, Juan had seemingly floated from church to church, first involved in a "Bible" church, then a Baptist church, and finally a Reformed church. He had even graduated from a

Reformed seminary. Reformed, Baptist, Evangelical—the names mattered little to him now. They all had one thing in common. They were all "Bible only" churches. They had all taught *"sola Scriptura"*; a teaching he now knew was hopelessly deficient. Deficient because the teaching itself cannot be found in the Bible. It was *that* truth that had ultimately coaxed him back; the cold, hard truth that *sola Scriptura* itself—the teaching that the Bible *alone* is our authority— is *itself* unbiblical. How ironic, he thought, that he had once traded the infallible security of being in the One True Church for the uncertainty of his own fallible interpretations of the Bible. That is, after all, what his ultimate authority had been—his own *private, fallible* understanding of the Bible. It was this very private judgment and private interpretation of the Bible that had produced so many different Protestant denominations in the first place. That principle, it seemed to him, resulted in nothing by uncertain chaos. How could anyone in that system have any kind of certitude that he was in the truth at all?

His newfound faith, on the other hand, was quite different. The Bible clearly taught that Jesus had founded His Church upon Peter, and that that Church was infallible. He knew from his reading of church history that the Roman Bishop was the successor of Peter, and that the Catholic Church was the true Church founded by Jesus Christ Himself. Since God endowed His Church with the charism of infallibility, he could therefore rest assured that the Catholic Church was not prone to doctrinal error. For the first time in his life he could have absolute certitude that what he believed was the truth, and that there was absolutely no need to second-guess the Catholic Church in any of its official teachings. That thought comforted him.

Juan allowed his mind to wander back over the events of the past few years while he waited for the driver. His decision to return to Rome had been a long time in the making, and the road had not been easy. He had lost many friends, and had nearly been disowned by some members of his own family whom he had personally "led to Christ" years before. He felt personally responsible for their current animosity toward the Church. After all, these family members had already been part of the true Church, and he had led them away from her. There was much reparation to be done for his misinformed actions toward them; and he resolved that, by God's grace, he would lead them back some day.

As a student at a Reformed Protestant seminary he had challenged his classmates and his professors alike on several issues about which he had serious questions. Questions such as, "Where does the Bible teach that the Bible *alone* is our authority?" Questions such as, "Where does the Bible provide us with a divine table of contents that would tell us which books should be included in the canon of Scripture?" And questions such as, "How can you be certain that *your* private interpretation of Scripture is correct when there are over 25,000 *other* denominations out there who claim that it is *their* private interpretation of Scripture that is correct? All of these denominations affirm *sola Scriptura*, and claim to derive their beliefs from the Bible alone. Yet they've all come to different conclusions on major doctrinal issues. How can *you* be absolutely certain that it is *your* church that is right on these issues and not some other church?"

All of these questions had been cleverly designed to expose the deficiency of the very "material principle" that had allowed the sixteenth-century Reformation to occur in the first place; namely, *sola Scriptura*. Juan smiled to himself as he recalled how his questions had always been met with an awkward silence on the part of his audience; fellow students and professors alike. He beamed with pride at his own theological acumen. The professors he had quizzed on these issues were not slackers, after all. They were some of the top Protestant theologians in the country. If these questions had only been asked in the days of the Reformation, the Reformation might never have occurred.

In fact, his notoriety and fame had preceded him. He had become something of a celebrity in the Catholic Church, even before his official entry. Word had spread quickly among Catholic apologetic circles that a seminary-trained Protestant "theologian" was about to convert to Catholicism. Okay, so he wasn't *exactly* a theologian. But if they wanted to call him a theologian, fine. The instant-celebrity status, he admitted, felt good. He had certainly not received this kind of recognition in any Protestant church. He had always wanted to be esteemed as a theologian; but never had he imagined that this esteem would come from Catholics! He momentarily allowed himself the pleasure of musing over his own future importance in the Church. If he had not been converted, would the Church today have a figurehead as capable as he for persuading Protestants to return to Rome? He had already convinced his good friend and "fellow theologian"—and former fellow seminarian— Gary Maverick, to follow in his footsteps and return to the Catholic Church, and Gary had agreed to do so. He wondered if perhaps in the future he might even become known as the person responsible for reversing the Reformation!

He heaved a sigh and chuckled inside. He glanced at his watch. In just twenty-five minutes he would be the guest of honor at the home of some new friends who had insisted on hosting a small gathering in celebration of his decision—but not before a quick stop by his own house for a change of clothes.

As the cab came into sight, Juan moved closer to the road, simultaneously lifting his left index finger in the air and tilting his head back slightly to signal the driver. The cab pulled in front of the church and stopped just beyond the bench in front of him. Juan gave the driver a wave and a smile as he noticed the familiar face of the person who had dropped him off at the church earlier that day. Juan climbed through the rear passenger-side door and closed it firmly behind him. As the cab moved into the street, Juan looked back one last time at the image in the stained-glass window. He felt moved as he thought of how much she had to suffer for him.

"Where to?" the cab driver asked in a gruff voice.

The image in the glass seemed to smile at him, filling him with a sense of well being. He felt his eyes begin to well up with tears.

"Going home, sir?" the cab driver asked again, this time with a bit more resolve. Juan tore his eyes away from the image in the glass, and attempted to gather his thoughts.

"Home?" Juan parroted, hoping the mere verbalization of the word would somehow focus him back to the conversation at hand.

"Yes sir, are you going home?" the driver reiterated, this time peering through the rear view mirror.

"*Going* home?" Juan responded with a chuckle. He was certain the driver had no idea of the significance those words held for him. The driver peered silently at Juan in the rear view mirror, waiting; seemingly at a loss as to how he might clarify the question further.

"*Going* home?" Juan repeated the phrase aloud, this time addressing himself. The smile on his face broadened. "I *am* home."

4. A Roman Catholic Challenge

THE EXPERIENCE of our fictitious character, Juan Scott, is nevertheless an all-too-real experience among former Protestants who have converted to Roman Catholicism. Indeed, our story is a composite based on the conversion stories of some of the more popular Roman Catholic apologists who converted to Rome from one Protestant denomination or the other. Most of them, at least from their accounting of events, were to some degree staunch "anti-Catholics" who battled Rome's "doctrines of demons" while simultaneously enjoying the theological status of "Protestant scholars" or "Protestant theologians," and who were "well-known" in Protestant circles.[3] In each case, the conversion was the result of a sudden realization that man is fallible and must engage in private interpretation of the Bible. This "private interpretation" activity is unnecessary for the Roman Catholic, it is argued, for he may safely submit his own fallible reasoning processes and consequent fallible interpretations to an infallible Church.

Earlier I made mention of a "Roman Catholic challenge" I had posted on my web site. For the Roman Catholic who argues this way, we issued the following challenge:

> Tell us how you came to decide that Rome was the "true" church without engaging in the very private judgment that you have already dismissed as illegitimate.

The significance of this challenge is this: Roman Catholic apologists claim that without an infallible interpreter, we, as Evangelicals, can never be certain about the correct interpretation of Scripture and church history. The best *we* can do in *our* situation is rely on our own *fallible* private judgment to pick what *we* think is the best interpretation among the many interpretations from which to choose.

However, this implies that if one decides on Rome as that choice, he must do so without engaging in the very private judgment that the Roman Catholic apologist has already told us is illegitimate. This means, for instance, that the Roman Catholic cannot appeal to his interpretation of Matthew 16, which he thinks identifies Peter as the first pope; nor to any other biblical passage for that matter, since appealing to *any* passage of Scripture would necessarily force the Roman Catholic to engage in private interpretation. Nor can he look down the annals of church history to find evidence that the churches granted primacy to the Roman bishop, for those writings *too* are subject to interpretation, and most church historians disagree with Rome's understanding of them. Hence, he would again be forced to engage in private judgment.

While reading through the many responses I received to this challenge question, I was struck by the fact that the Roman Catholic contestants who responded tended to miss this point rather consistently. The challenge question gives explicit instructions not to engage in private judgment in the response. Yet, without exception, every contestant engaged in the very private judgment that Roman Catholics insist is illegitimate for Protestants. One contestant had this to say:

> This question has a false premise because the Catholic Church does not condemn private judgments. It condemns only private judgments which contradict the official teaching of the Church, and the judgment that the Catholic Church is true does not contradict that.

The contestant is of course arguing in a circle. To assert that "only private judgments which contradict" official Roman teaching is condemned by Rome is to assert a truism that first assumes what it later seeks to prove. Well of course Rome condemns *only* those private judgments that contradict its official teaching; but that hardly answers the question. Obviously, any system could argue that way with just as much (or perhaps more accurately, just as little) legitimacy! The Watchtower Society, for instance, sees private judgment that leads you to become a Jehovah's Witness as perfectly legitimate, but condemns any private judgment that leads you away from the Watchtower Society. How comforting it is to know that Rome allows me to engage in private judgment—so long as that private judgment does not contradict what Rome teaches!

The bottom line is, this contestant has confused the principle upon which he operated to get to Rome (namely, private judgment) with the resulting decision (namely, choosing Rome). The fact is, he had to engage in the very same principle of private judgment that we all must use to decide among the various options; namely, a thinking, objective reasoning process, apart from reliance upon the system to which he would eventually subscribe. But it is that very same principle of private judgment that leads him *to* Rome and others of us *away from* Rome. Certainly Rome condemns the decision we reached, but she cannot condemn the principle we used to reach that decision, since it is the very same principle that all Roman Catholics *must* use to decide that Rome is the "true" church. The Roman Catholic cannot introduce a double standard at this point and still be consistent.

All of the Roman Catholic responses to this challenge question that I received were blatant displays of private interpretation. Many appealed to their own understanding of this or that biblical text, or to this or that document of church history—the very thing the challenge question instructed them not to do. At least one of the contestants was honest enough to admit that we must use private judgment to decide that Rome is the true church, but then suggested that this must be acknowledged as an exception.

While I was thrilled to see at least one Roman Catholic admit the obvious double standard, it is simply gratuitous to suggest that private judgment is sufficient to interpret Scripture and church history to determine whether Rome is the true church, but *in*sufficient to interpret Scripture and church history once we either accept or reject Rome. After all, in order to arrive at the conclusion that Rome is the true church, we must first compare Rome to Scripture and church history; hence, we must first engage in private interpretation of these things before choosing Rome. But if our private interpretation of Scripture and church history is sufficient to inform us that Rome is the true church, how is it that that same private interpretation is suddenly rendered deficient once we either get to Rome or reject Rome?

Far from the Roman Catholic notion of these things, Paul, in Galatians 1:8–9 expressly instructs us to use private judgment. He tells us not to believe "anyone" who comes preaching a gospel that is "different" than that contained in the original apostolic deposit. Verse 8 of this passage says this: "But even if we or an angel from heaven should preach a gospel other than the one we preached to you, let him be eternally condemned!"

All we need do is compare the teaching of the original apostolic deposit (found in Scripture) to the teaching of any supposed "religious authority" to see whether the message is the same. What we find when we compare that original deposit to Rome is that the message is not the same, and so we must reject Rome. Paul is not asking us in such a case simply to submit our fallible judgments to the teachings of a magisterial "Religious Authority"; indeed, by using the phrase "even if we," Paul places even the apostles themselves in the category of those to be rejected if the message they preach does not square with the original deposit. It is clear that Paul assumes here that we should judge *all* supposed "religious authorities" by comparing their gospel to the original deposit. Hence, Paul *commands* us to use private judgment.

This passage makes absolutely no sense in the Roman Catholic scheme in which we simply submit ourselves to the Pope and resign ourselves to the notion that if there seems to be a conflict between Rome's teaching and that of the Scriptures, it must be due to the complete failure of our reasoning faculties, rather than due to the inaccuracy of that teaching. On the contrary, Paul assumes we will be engaging in private judgment and interpretation of the original gospel to test the authenticity of any other rival gospel that may come along.

The burden of this first challenge question has been for the Roman Catholic to do the following: Show us a method of reasoning that forces everyone to arrive at the same conclusion regarding Rome's claim to be the true church. All of the proposed methods mentioned by the Roman Catholics who responded include the use of private judgment on the part of the respondent. This, of course, must be disallowed. One cannot use private judgment and interpretation to sift through the historical and biblical data in order to arrive at Rome, and then (1) view that very principle as illegitimate for everyone else who uses it and arrives elsewhere, and (2) view that very principle as illegitimate for himself once he has arrived. Conversely, if one's reasoning faculties are sufficient to interpret the historical and biblical data before coming to Rome, and the seeker uses them to arrive at Rome, those same reasoning faculties cannot suddenly be deemed deficient once he has arrived. Moreover, if they were sufficient for the person who finally ended up at Rome, they can be no less sufficient for those of us who, viewing the same historical and biblical data, end up rejecting Rome.

At the end of the day, the Roman Catholic argument fails on the basis that it is self-refuting. The body of literature that we are told plainly identifies the "infallible interpreter" for us (namely, Scripture and church history) is the very body of literature that we are later told we cannot understand *without* that "infallible interpreter." Obviously, such a system contains internal contradictions at the most fundamental level, and is therefore inadequate for laying a sound epistemological foundation for truth.

5. A Layman's Handbook for Roman Catholic Apologetics

WELCOME TO *Catholic Responses 101*, the final word on how to answer Protestant and anti-Catholic objections to the faith of the One True Church! When discussing issues of authority with a Protestant, keep in mind the following guidelines:

1. The Roman Catholic Church is infallible!

2. All of the writings of the church fathers that *can* be marshaled in support of Roman Catholic beliefs *should* be marshaled in support of Roman Catholic beliefs. These church fathers, although perhaps not infallible in everything they teach, must be viewed as making up the *ordinary* magisterium.

3. All the writings of the early church fathers that seem to contradict these teachings fall under one of the following categories:
   a. They are fallible.
   b. They are heretical.
   c. They are misunderstood and misinterpreted by Protestants (assume this last category unless one of the other two doesn't call into question Rome's infallibility).

4. No *official* Roman Catholic teaching has ever changed, and all Roman Catholic dogmas have been held unswervingly by the true Church throughout the centuries.

5. In the case of a Roman Catholic teaching that can't clearly be found in the early church, that teaching was never-

theless "held from the beginning" anyway; and, amazingly enough, it simultaneously "developed" over time.

6. Roman Catholics today who disagree with Rome's "official" teachings are in disobedience or apostasy. "Official" is always to be defined by the conservative minority branch of Roman Catholicism.

7. Just because there are disagreements among modern Roman Catholics as to the *meaning* of these "official" teachings, this does not imply that any official Roman Catholic teaching has ever changed. Always assume that the conservative minority interpretation of "official" Roman Catholic teaching is the correct one.

8. Not all popes were infallible in all they taught. Some teachings of popes were stated by them while they were speaking as "private theologians." Hence, any papal teaching that apparently contradicts current Roman Catholic teaching must have been made by a pope who was speaking as a "private theologian," rather than in his official role as pope.

9. Reiterate #1 above as many times as is necessary.

What's Good for the Goose

What would happen if we were to apply this politics-as-usual rationale of Roman Catholic apologists to Evangelicalism? How would it change the face of Evangelical apologetics? How different would our approach be? The following are some suggested "tongue-in-cheek" guidelines for discussing issues of authority with a Roman Catholic:

1. The Westminster Confession is infallible!

2. All the church fathers that *can* be marshaled in support of Evangelical beliefs *should* be marshaled in support of Evangelical beliefs. These church fathers, although perhaps not infallible in everything they teach, must be

considered as making up the *ordinary* Evangelical magisterium.

3. All church fathers who seem to contradict the teachings of the Westminster Confession fall under one of the following categories:
   a. They are fallible.
   b. They are heretical.
   c. They are misunderstood/misinterpreted by Roman Catholics (assume this last category unless one of the other two doesn't call into question Evangelical infallibility).

4. No *official* Evangelical teaching has ever changed, and all Evangelical teachings have been held unswervingly by the true "remnant" church throughout the centuries.

5. In the case of an Evangelical teaching that can't clearly be found in the early church, that teaching was nevertheless "held from the beginning" anyway; and, amazingly enough, it simultaneously "developed" over time.

6. Protestants today who disagree with the Westminster Confession are in disobedience or apostasy.

7. Just because there are disagreements among modern Evangelicals as to the *meaning* of these teachings, this does not imply that any official Evangelical teaching has ever changed. Always assume that the conservative interpretation of "official" Evangelical teaching is the correct one.

8. Not all the Reformers' teachings were infallible. Some teachings of Calvin and Luther were stated by them while they were speaking as "private theologians." Hence, any Reformer's teaching that apparently contradicts current Evangelical teaching must have been made by a Reformer who was speaking as a "private theologian," rather than in his official role as a Reformer.

9. Reiterate #1 above as many times as is necessary.

How much easier our job as Evangelical apologists would be if we were simply to adopt the methodology of our Roman Catholic friends! Honesty, of course, compels us to move in other directions. This Roman Catholic apologetic methodology is perhaps at its worst in online Internet discussion forums. I have included below the comments of Jason Engwer, a colleague of mine and arguably one of the best online Evangelical apologists today. In his dealings with on-line Roman Catholic lay-apologists, he has made several humorous, yet insightful observations regarding the dubious methodology used to establish Rome's claim to authority over all of Christendom. Many of us who deal with Roman Catholic apologists on a regular basis regarding these issues can attest to the fact that what you are about to read is very real indeed! I leave you with Jason Engwer's list in its entirety:

1. We can't understand the Scriptures apart from the inter-pretations of the Roman Catholic Church, but we must interpret the Scriptures ourselves to discover that the Roman Catholic Church has been given this authority.

2. Roman Catholic doctrine is valid regardless of whether the apostles or anybody living near the time of the apostles taught it. If a doctrine such as the Immaculate Conception or papal infallibility is not taught by anybody in the earliest centuries of Christianity, and there's no evidence that the apostles taught it, and many early sources actually deny it, the doctrine should be believed anyway on the basis of a vague and unverifiable "development of doctrine."

3. The teachings of the Roman Catholic Church have been held all along by the Christian church, but it's unreason-able to expect Catholics to document this, because, after all, the beliefs didn't exist early on. They developed over time.

4. If the Roman Catholic Church teaches that a doctrine such as the papacy or transubstantiation has "always" been held by the Christian church, it's ridiculous for Evangeli-

cals to expect Catholics to have to defend that claim. Instead, they should only have to defend the concept that something vaguely similar to the papacy or transubstantiation was believed early on. It's not right to expect Catholics to defend what their denomination teaches. They should only be expected to defend something that's vaguely similar to what their denomination teaches.

5. Even though Evangelicals advocate *sola Scriptura*, and they don't claim that the church fathers were "apostolic successors," they're just as responsible as Catholics are to show that their beliefs are in line with those of the church fathers.

6. Even if a passage of Scripture says nothing about governmental authority, a succession of Roman bishops, etc., it's reasonable to assume that the passage is referring to a papacy. It doesn't matter if the "keys" mentioned in this passage (Matthew 16) can be interpreted in a number of ways. It doesn't matter if this passage says nothing about governmental supremacy. It doesn't matter if the passage says nothing about a succession of Roman bishops. As long as a passage uses terminology into which it's possible to read a Roman Catholic interpretation, then all of the Roman Catholic Church's claims to authority are thereby validated. This only applies to passages about Peter and Mary, however. You can't read these things into passages about Paul or John, for example. But if we're dealing with a passage relating to Peter or Mary, then the sky is the limit as far as speculation is concerned. You can claim that Matthew 16:18 teaches a papacy, Luke 1:28 teaches an immaculate conception, Luke 22:32 teaches papal infallibility, John 19:26 teaches that Mary is Mother of the Church and dispenser of all grace, etc. That there are many other possible interpretations of these passages, and that there's no way to validate the Catholic interpretations, is irrelevant.

7. The Roman Catholic Church can err and contradict itself as much as it wants to (anti-Semitism, selling indulgences, Popes and councils contradicting one another, etc.), yet still be "Infallible Mother Church." If anybody brings up these errors, we need to either "put the past behind us" or realize that every error of the Roman Catholic Church is "unofficial." There's no definite, consistent criteria by which to determine which actions of the RCC are "official" and which are "unofficial," but it's generally a matter of anything obviously erroneous being "unofficial." So we must wait to see whether the Roman Catholic Church is correct on an issue before deciding whether the Roman Catholic Church is acting "officially." The Roman Catholic Church is acting officially only when it's correct. And since the Roman Catholic Church has always been correct every time it's acted officially, we should be impressed with this amazing record of infallibility.

6. A Second Roman Catholic Challenge

RETURNING TO our Roman Catholic challenge, the second challenge question I posted on my web site was a follow-up question to the first. It reads this way:

> Demonstrate that those religious systems that follow 'Scripture plus an Infallible Interpreter' are more unified in their beliefs than those religious systems that follow *sola Scriptura*.

The intent of this challenge question is to reveal the false comparison that Roman Catholic apologists make when issuing their "25,000 denominations" argument. The comments of one contestant who responded to the challenge will serve to illustrate my point. He writes this:

> The beliefs of such systems (i.e., infallible interpreters) are generally more easily determined, (for instance, read the Catechism of the Catholic Church). [In comparison] there is no single Protestant Catechism. Also the Catholic Church has only a few major unhealed schisms, whereas there are tens of thousands of other churches based on 'sola Scriptura' which continue to fragment daily.

This contestant, as all the contestants who attempted to respond to this question, has misunderstood the challenge. First, to compare the Catechism of the Catholic Church to a non-existent, "single" Protestant Catechism is to miss the point entirely and to compare apples and oranges. The contestant is comparing a single entity within the

43

collective body of entities that maintain we must subscribe to the Bible plus an infallible interpreter (which we'll call "system 1") to the entire collective body of entities that maintain we must subscribe to the Bible alone (which we'll call "system 2"). In order to make a fair comparison, the contestant must select one of the entities within system 1 (say, Roman Catholicism) and compare it to only one of the entities within system 2 (say, the Reformed Baptist church). I dare say, there is much more doctrinal unity within the Reformed Baptist church than there is in the Roman Catholic church.

Second, the "tens of thousands" of churches (to which the contestant refers) that subscribe to *sola Scriptura* are far more unified than the tens of thousands of churches that subscribe to the Bible plus an infallible interpreter. For instance, the Evangelical Free church and the Reformed Baptist church are far more doctrinally unified than are the Roman Catholic church and the Mormon church. The first two believe in *sola Scriptura*, and as a result have come to very similar beliefs—and embrace each other as brothers; while the latter two believe in the Bible plus an infallible interpreter, and as a result disagree on almost every point of doctrine—and reject each other as heretics! Obviously, the principle of "Bible plus an infallible interpreter" creates nothing but doctrinal chaos and anarchy. Indeed, one could pick at random half a dozen belief systems that subscribe to *sola Scriptura* and they would invariably be more unified than any half dozen belief systems that subscribe to the Bible plus an infallible interpreter. Moreover, there are absolutely no two belief systems within the "Bible plus an infallible interpreter" camp that embrace each other as brothers; whereas in the case of the *sola Scriptura* camp, everyone—with very few exceptions—embraces everyone else as brothers. That, I submit, is true biblical unity.

Let's look at another contestant's response:

> The Church's official teachers—the pope and the bishops united with him—have never changed any doctrine. Although there are certainly dissenters within her midst, the official teaching of the Church has remained constant for 2000 years, and is the same in every part of the world.

This contestant, as the last one, has misunderstood the challenge. This misunderstanding is most likely due to the fact that the false comparison raised by Roman Catholic apologists between the one denomination of Rome vs. the many denominations of Protestantism is such a deeply entrenched fallacy in the Roman Catholic mind that it is difficult for the contestant to escape its clutches. In fact, the challenge asks the Roman Catholic to demonstrate that the unity among *all* institutions that hold to Scripture *plus* an infallible interpreter (Rome, the Eastern Orthodox Church, the Watchtower Society, Mormonism, etc.) is greater than the unity among all institutions that hold to Scripture alone. This he cannot do. Hence, the challenge question demonstrates the fallacy of the Roman Catholic apologist who argues that since Protestantism has over "25,000" denominations then its guiding principle (namely, *sola Scriptura*) must be a "blueprint for anarchy." That argument is based entirely on the false premise that the one denomination of Rome should be compared to the many denominations of Protestantism. The argument as such compares a *rule of faith* (namely, *sola Scriptura*) to a *denomination* (namely, Rome). This is obviously a false comparison.

What the Roman Catholic apologist needs to do instead is one of two things: Either (1) compare his rule of faith (namely, Scripture plus an infallible interpreter) to our rule of faith (namely, *sola Scriptura*); or (2) compare a single denomination that adheres to his rule of faith (such as Rome or Mormonism or the Watchtower Society, etc.) to a single denomination that adheres to our rule of faith (such as Reformed Baptists, or Evangelical Free, or PCA, etc.). When a true comparison is made between "sola Scriptura" *as a rule of faith* and "Scripture plus an infallible interpreter" *as a rule of faith*, or between one denomination that adheres to the *one* rule of faith and one denomination that adheres to the *other* rule of faith, it becomes abundantly clear that Rome utterly fails the unity test. For when one randomly selects, say, any five religious systems that follow Scripture alone as their rule of faith and compares them to any five religious systems that follow Scripture *plus* an infallible interpreter as their rule of faith, it is beyond dispute that the former group will be much more unified than the latter—that we who follow *sola*

Scriptura will be much more unified in our beliefs than those who follow Scripture plus an infallible interpreter.

Many Roman Catholics are under the false impression that only the Roman Catholic church and the Eastern Orthodox Church claim the principle of Scripture plus an infallible interpreter, and that those two churches are much more unified than Protestants. Obviously, this is incorrect, since there are tens of thousands of religious systems that claim Scripture *plus* an infallible interpreter, including the tens of thousands of cults that exist in the world today. Yet, the differences even between Rome and the Eastern Orthodox Church are much greater than the differences between, say, Reformed Baptist churches and Evangelical Free churches. Indeed, even though post-Vatican II Rome officially views the Eastern Orthodox Church as "brothers," the Eastern Orthodox Church still believes Rome to be heretical and lost.

While Roman Catholic apologists are fond of pointing out all of the doctrinal differences that result from the principle of *sola Scriptura*, this challenge question has shown that the "rule of faith" by which Rome operates is a much more disunifying principle than is the rule of faith by which Evangelicals operate. Obviously, any two randomly selected religious systems that adhere to *sola Scriptura* as a rule of faith will invariably be more unified than any two randomly selected religious systems that adhere to "Scripture plus an infallible interpreter" as a rule of faith. Certainly, if one simply compares Rome (which is only *one* adherent of the one rule of faith) to Protestantism (which consists of *all* adherents of the other rule of faith), one may see more unity in the first than in the second. However, as we have already shown, such a comparison is a false comparison since it compares "apples to oranges." The Roman Catholic who appeals to such an argument says more about his own unwillingness to engage in rational thought and to understand epistemological foundations, than he does about real comparisons.

7. Show Me the Way To Go Rome

DEBBIE REACHED across the table and took Nancy's hand. "But just look at all the unnecessary confusion it has caused," Debbie asserted, and then added, "My goodness, even Martin Luther ended up regretting formulating his principle of sola Scriptura because of all the denominations it resulted in."

Debbie could sense she was getting through to Nancy. Nancy sat motionless, her eyes locked on one small area of the tabletop. Finally, she broke her silence.

"I don't know, Debbie," Nancy said warily, pulling her hand away from Debbie's. Her voice sounded uncertain, and Debbie knew she had more work to do.

"But Nancy, you know it's true—you *know* it is," Debbie insisted, leaning forward in her chair, her hand patting the tabletop in an exaggerated motion. "If everyone is left to interpret the Bible on his own—which is what is occurring in Protestantism—it creates nothing but doctrinal divisions. There are already over 25,000 denominations today, and even *those* are continuing to fragment as we speak!"

Debbie could feel the excitement building within her—excitement that had caused her voice to raise slightly and her rate of speech to increase. This kind of conversation always had this effect on her. She had to be careful because, in her experience, people tended to withdraw when she did this. She had blown it in the past when speaking to other friends about this issue, and she didn't want to make that same mistake with Nancy. She leaned back in her chair, took a deep breath and spoke in a calm, easy, deliberate tone.

"Imagine how wonderful it would be not to have to worry and wonder about whether or not you really are in the truth," Debbie

47

suggested. *"That's* what is so great about coming home to Rome," she added, "knowing for certain that you believe all the right things, and not ever having to worry about that again!"

Nancy remained silent, her expression emotionless. Debbie sensed that perhaps this had been enough for one day. She didn't want to risk becoming overbearing and driving Nancy away.

"Tell you what," Debbie broke the silence, "Why don't you just sleep on this, and if you're up for talking more tomorrow, we can."

Nancy continued to gaze at the tabletop, lips pursed. She slowly nodded to indicate her agreement. The two women rose out of their chairs and walked silently together toward the sliding-glass door. Debbie placed her hand on the back of Nancy's arm and guided her outside.

"I hope I didn't offend you by any of this," Debbie stated, a tone of genuine concern in her voice.

Nancy seemed to snap out of her trance for the first time in what seemed like hours. She laughed and placed her hand on Debbie's free arm. "Heavens no; of course not," Nancy assured her with a smile, then added, "I'm sorry I gave you that impression. I get like this when I'm thinking things through."

"Oh good," Debbie replied, relieved she had not overstepped her bounds, "I'd hate to think I said too much."

"Oh, not at all!" Nancy said, tightening her grip slightly on Debbie's arm. "In fact, I do have a question for you before I go."

"Of course," Debbie replied, excited at Nancy's renewed interest in the subject, "What is it?"

"Well, I was just wondering," Nancy began, her eyes and forehead drawn together quizzically. "You've said that we can't be certain we are in the truth by looking to the Bible alone because the principle of *sola Scriptura*, or 'Bible only,' has resulted in countless denominations, right?"

"Yes, right," Debbie affirmed, nodding.

Nancy continued, "And you've said that the reason this happens is because each of us is exercising his or her own private judgment about what the Bible and church history teaches, right?"

"Yes, right," Debbie repeated, again nodding.

"Which means that we need an infallible interpreter to be certain we've rightly understood the Bible and church history," Nancy concluded.

"Exactly!," Debbie exclaimed, exaggerating her nod this time, pleased that Nancy had understood the ramifications of *sola Scriptura* so well.

"Okay, I just wanted to be clear that I understood you," Nancy said calmly, then added, "How do you know for certain that Rome is that infallible interpreter?"

Debbie paused. She turned her head slightly while continuing to make eye contact with Nancy. "I'm not sure I understand what you mean," she said, inviting Nancy to elaborate. "Rome has a 2,000-year old pedigree. It is the church that was founded on Peter by our Lord Jesus in Matthew 16."

"But," Nancy responded, "if I can't trust my own ability to understand the Bible and church history, then how do I know I'm interpreting Matthew 16 and that '2,000-year pedigree' correctly? How can I be certain that it is *Rome* who is God's *true* infallible interpreter? How can I ever be certain that the *true* infallible interpreter is not the Eastern Orthodox Church, or the Mormon Church, or the Watchtower Society, or any one of the tens of thousands of cults that exist today? *All* of them *claim* to be God's infallible interpreter. How can I be certain that once I have chosen Rome over all the others, I have actually made the right choice?"

Debbie was stunned as she allowed the full impact of Nancy's questions to come home. She had never even heard these questions before, much less thought them through. When she had come to the conclusion years before that Rome was the true Church, she had always prided herself on the fact that *that* decision had been the fruit of years of personal Bible study and personal investigation of the writings of the Church Fathers. She had always been confident that an examination of the Bible and Church history could lead any honest seeker to the true Church of Rome. Yet, she was also telling Evangelicals on a daily basis that their own private reading of the Bible and Church history was not to be trusted, and that they needed Rome's infallible interpreter to come to a correct understanding of them.

Any answer she gave to Nancy would reveal that she did indeed rely on her own fallible private judgment and interpretation to determine that Rome was the true Church and that the rest were not. Indeed, how *did* she know for certain that Rome was the true church without relying on her own private understanding of the Bible and church history? She was speechless.

"And when you think about it," Nancy continued, sensing that Debbie's answer was not forthcoming, "as many differences as there may be among Evangelical denominations, there are many more—and much greater—differences among all the competing 'infallible interpreters' in the world. The real difference between your 'infallible interpreter' principle and my 'Bible only' principle is that nearly all of us who hold to the 'Bible only' principle freely embrace each other as Christians, while all of you who hold to the 'infallible interpreter' principle exclude each other as heretics. Seems to me there is much more unity—not to mention safety and certainty of being in truth!—in the 'Bible only' camp than there is in the 'infallible interpreter camp.' I mean, I can belong to this 'Bible only' denomination or to that one and still know I am a Christian who is going to heaven. But you must pledge your allegiance to only *one* 'infallible interpreter' to the exclusion of all others. And if you happen to pick the wrong one, you risk eternal damnation as a heretic. There are tens of thousands of 'infallible interpreters' out there, each with thousands, or even millions, of followers. All of them claim that you cannot rightly understand the Bible and church history without their help. What are the chances that *you* just happened to pick the right one, and that all the millions of followers of the tens of thousands of other 'infallible interpreters' just happened to pick the wrong one? Since you believe you can't trust your own ability to interpret the Bible and church history, isn't any decision to choose *one* of these 'infallible interpreters' over all the others simply a blind leap in the dark?"

Debbie's head reeled. She felt as though the wind had been knocked right out of her. She frantically searched her mind for an answer to this. She had always considered herself to be an informed Catholic. She had read all the best Catholic apologetics books available to her. She had listened to countless hours of taped lectures by the top Catholic apologists in the country. She had even listened to debate tapes between Catholic apologists and Evangelical apologists—and had even memorized the Catholic answers she had learned from them. But none of these things had prepared her for *this* conversation.

"Oh well," Nancy chimed in, sensing the awkward silence, and not wishing to put Debbie on the spot, "Why don't we just *both* sleep on it tonight? We can talk about it again tomorrow if you'd like."

"Yeah, sleep on it," Debbie muttered, staring at the wall, only semi-conscious of what she had just said.

"Bye," Nancy exclaimed enthusiastically, leaving the house in her usual animated way.

"Yeah, see ya," Debbie mumbled, her eyes following Nancy as she walks away. She continued to watch as Nancy climbed into her car, backed out of the driveway, and drove off. She continued to stare into the distance long after Nancy's car disappeared from sight; her head still reeling from the conversation she had just had; her mind racing…thinking…wondering…questioning.

8. A Third Roman Catholic Challenge

RETURNING once again to our Roman Catholic challenge, the final epistemological question that I posed in the challenge reads as follows:

> Without engaging in private judgment and interpretation, demonstrate how you can be certain that you chose the "true" church from among all the other so-called "true" churches that say you cannot rightly understand the Bible and church history without their help, such as the Eastern Orthodox church, the Watchtower Society, Mormonism, and every other cult that exists.

This final challenge question is a follow-up to our previous challenge question. The intent of the question is this: Since, as we have shown in the previous challenge question, those religious systems that hold to the principle of "Scripture plus an infallible interpreter" depart from each other to such a great extent doctrinally as to be mutually exclusive, the Roman Catholic must choose *one* of these systems over all the others in order to be certain he has the true gospel, and hence eternal life. In other words, it asks the Roman Catholic to define a method for choosing among the tens of thousands of competing religious systems that claim an infallible interpreter. Note well that this stipulation does not apply to those religious systems that hold to the principle of *sola Scriptura*. As a *sola Scriptura* adherent, I can walk into any Evangelical church and find the true gospel. The fact that there may be a handful of *sola Scriptura* churches that do not hold to the true gospel no more militates against the validity of *sola Scriptura* than does the fact that there are some blind people in the world militate against the validity of the eye.

All of the contestants who responded to this final question, without exception, again did the very thing that the challenge question instructed them not to do; namely, they relied on their fallible, private understanding of Scripture and church history to make this decision. The reason that the challenge question instructs the contestants to exclude the use of private judgment and interpretation to determine which religious system is correct in its understanding of these things, is because every single competing infallible interpreter claims that you cannot understand Scripture and church history without its help. It is circular reasoning to start with Rome's understanding of these things and then judge all other religious systems by looking through Rome-colored glasses; but this is precisely what the Roman Catholic apologist *must* do, and indeed what all the contestants who responded to this final challenge question in fact *did* do. The Roman Catholic apologist consistently engages in circular reasoning to defend Roman Catholic authority. That, I submit, is the *only* way Roman Catholics *can* argue; and we have seen it demonstrated time and again by their inability to answer these three simple challenge questions.

This final challenge question concludes our inquiry into the epistemology of Roman Catholic apologists. Epistemology essentially asks the question, "How do you know what you claim to know?" Roman Catholic apologists typically argue that we must submit our fallible opinions to an infallible Roman Catholic church. But none of them explains how he knows that Rome is indeed infallible without relying on his own fallible opinion that Rome is infallible. What is worse is that it doesn't even seem to occur to these apologists that this underlying question completely undermines their previous claim that private judgment and interpretation is an illegitimate principle; for each one of them must rely on this very same "illegitimate" principle several times before he can arrive at Rome.

The final arbiter, for every single human being, is—and must be—private judgment and reliance on one's own fallible reasoning faculties. There is simply no way around that fact. If someone decides to use those fallible reasoning faculties to arrive at Rome, he cannot then claim that those same reasoning faculties are illegitimate for everyone else who does not arrive at Rome—nor can he claim objective "safety" or "certitude" just because he thinks he has made the right decision. Bear in mind that even the decision to trust Rome as an infallible guide is *itself* a fallible decision, based on a private reading of Scripture and history. Once he arrives at Rome, the Roman Catholic cannot then claim that he has an advantage because he has an infallible interpreter while we Evangelicals are left to our own devices.

Any Roman Catholic who argues this way (and unfortunately there are all too many of them) has engaged in private judgment on at least three critical levels: (1) he has fallibly decided that there should be an infallible interpreter, (2) he has fallibly misread the Scriptures and history to conclude that there is an infallible interpreter, and (3) he has fallibly decided that Rome is that infallible interpreter while rejecting the tens of thousands of other competing religious authorities, all of which demand he submit to their "infallible interpreter" instead. Obviously, any "certitude" that a Roman Catholic thinks he has because he has submitted his "private judgment" to the supposed "authority" of Rome can only be as certain as the fallible decision he made in choosing Rome. Rome has claimed to be an infallible interpreter, and the Roman Catholic has fallibly decided to believe that claim.

Earlier we were asked by our Roman Catholic interlocutor how we can be certain we are in the true church if everyone is left to his or her own private judgment and interpretation. The answer is really twofold. First, as we have already shown, God commands us to use our own reasoning faculties to compare the gospel of any religious system to the true gospel as originally given (Gal 1:6–9). According to this passage, we are not even to believe a known apostle if his message conflicts with the original deposit, much less someone claiming to be his successor! This passage simply assumes that we have the ability to make this comparison, and hence the ability to know the true gospel. Once we know the true gospel (by reading the original deposit), and comply with its demands ("believe and be saved"), we may safely count ourselves among the elect of God.

Second, one of the reasons we have this ability to know the true gospel from error is that God, by the illumination of his Holy Spirit, has ensured that none of his elect will be deceived by serious error. In Matt 24:24, Jesus says: "False prophets will arise to deceive even the elect—if that were possible," indicating that it is not possible. In 1 John 2:20–27, John writes to ordinary Christians when he says: "you have an anointing from the Holy One, and all of you know the truth…you do not need anyone to teach you."

What that boils down to is that the elect of God will always believe essential tenets of the faith. What are the "essential" tenets of the faith? Well, in short, there is really no need to define them if, as we have already seen, the elect automatically have a propensity to believe them when they hear them.

Objectively, then, one need only compare the common beliefs within Evangelicalism to arrive at that list. Included here is belief in God as creator of all, the Trinity, the deity of Christ, the love of Christ, the work of Christ alone in our salvation, the intercessory work of Christ, the high-priesthood of Christ, the finality of the salvific work of Christ, the person, work and deity of the Holy Spirit, the illumination of the Holy Spirit in understanding the truth, the convicting work of the Holy Spirit in the life of the sinner, the existence of angels, the fall of Satan, the work and wiles of Satan, the gospel message of salvation by grace through faith alone; the forgiveness of sins by belief in this gospel, the principle of Adam's sin transferred to us so that "all sinned," the conscious and eternal blessedness of those who believe, the conscious and eternal punishment of those who don't believe, the authority of the church, the final authority of Scripture alone as a rule of faith binding on the conscience of the believer, the inerrancy and infallibility of the Scriptures, the unity of the Scriptures, the physical return of Christ, the bodily resurrection of Christ, the resurrection of the body of the believer, etc. I have listed only those beliefs that I could think of off the top of my head; a much fuller list could no doubt be compiled with a little more thought.

The point is, while Roman Catholics consistently focus on areas of disagreement among Evangelicals (as though they have none of their own—an assumption we have shown to be completely in error), they are, in fact, focusing only on areas of non-essential beliefs. For instance, one of the areas of disagreement to which Roman Catholics point is the exact nature of the Lord's Supper. Do we believe in consubstantiation (as with the Lutherans), a spiritual presence of Christ (as do most Reformed Christians), or a strictly symbolic presence of Christ (as do most other denominations)? Or, in the issue of baptism, do we believe in baptizing infants or believers only? The answer is—and this is important—*it just doesn't matter* because these are not matters of essential, binding belief. If they were, we Evangelicals would be rejecting each other as heretics.

The fact that we're not assigning each other to hell indicates that we recognize the nonessential character of these types of beliefs. The Bible tells us that the bread of the Lord's Supper is somehow Christ's body. Just how it is Christ's body is a matter of theological speculation. Don't misunderstand me; I am not for a minute suggesting that these are unimportant issues; nor that all views are equally strong. Only that where the Scriptures are silent (or nearly silent), there can be no essential belief—just as where there is no law there can be no transgression (Rom 4:15). In such a case, the principle of Rom 14:5 applies: "each one should be fully convinced in his own mind." Are there disagreements among Evangelicals? You bet—and there is no need to deny those differences in dialogue with a Roman Catholic. Are these disagreements *essential* disagreements? That's not even possible. No one who is the elect of God can be deceived in essential beliefs; which necessarily implies that any disagreements among Evangelicals cannot be disagreements over essential matters. That all Evangelicals agree with this principle is borne out by the fact that all Evangelicals, regardless of denominational affiliation, embrace one another as brothers in Christ. That there may be spurious, contentious groups that claim the principle of *sola Scriptura* and that disown the rest of us does not militate against the principle that I've outlined. If they do not believe in what we as Evangelicals have decided are essential beliefs, then they are not Evangelicals and, hence, are not true Christians. If they do subscribe to those beliefs but shun the rest of us who believe likewise, then they are divisive and are in turn to be shunned according to Rom 16:17–19, as well as other passages.

In short, Evangelicalism is the true church, and that is arrived at though the objective and collective interpretation of the Scriptures themselves.

9. How Many Denominations?

THROUGHOUT this book we have examined the Roman Catholic apologist's primary argument against *sola Scriptura* and Protestantism; namely, that *sola Scriptura* produces doctrinal anarchy as is witnessed in the 25,000 Protestant denominations extant today. We have all along assumed the soundness of the premise that in fact there *are* 25,000 Protestant denominations; and we have shown that even if this figure is correct, the Roman Catholic argument falls to the ground since it compares apples to oranges. We have just one more small detail to address before we can close; namely, the *correctness* of the infamous 25,000-Protestant-denominations figure itself.

When this figure first surfaced among Roman Catholic apologists, it started at 20,000 Protestant denominations, grew to 23,000 Protestant denominations, then to 25,000 Protestant denominations, and finally to the current number (as of this writing) of well over 33,000 Protestant denominations. These days, many Roman Catholic apologists feel at liberty simply to calculate a daily rate of growth (based on their previous adherence to the original benchmark figure of 20,000) that they can then use as a basis for projecting just how many Protestant denominations there were, or will be, in any given year. But from whence does this figure originate?

I have posed this question over and over again to many different Roman Catholic apologists, none of whom were able to verify the source with certainty. In most cases, one Roman Catholic apologist would claim he obtained the figure from another Roman Catholic apologist. When I would ask the latter Roman Catholic apologist about the figure, it was not uncommon for that apologist to point to the former apologist as *his* source for the figure, creating a circle with no actual beginning. I have long suspected that, whatever the source might be, the words "denomination" and "Protestant" were being defined in a way that most of us would reject.

I have only recently been able to locate the source of this figure. I say *the* source because in fact there is only *one* source that mentions this figure independently. All other secondary sources (to which Roman Catholics sometimes make appeal) ultimately cite the same original source. That source is David A. Barrett's *World Christian Encyclopedia: A Comparative Survey of Churches and Religions in the Modern World A.D. 1900–2000.*[4] This work is both comprehensive and painstakingly detailed; and its contents are quite enlightening. However, the reader who turns to this work for validation of the Roman Catholic 25,000-Protestant-denomination argument will be sadly disappointed. What follows is a synopsis of what Barrett's work in this area *really* says.

First, Barrett, writing in 1982, does indeed cite a figure of 20,780 denominations in 1980, and projects that there would be as many as 22,190 denominations by 1985. This represents an increase of approximately 270 new denominations each year.[5] What the Roman Catholic who cites this figure does not tell us (most likely because he does not know) is that most of these denominations are *non*-Protestant.

Barrett identifies seven major ecclesiastical "blocs" under which these 22,190 distinct denominations fall:[6] (1) Roman Catholicism, which accounts for 223 denominations; (2) Protestant, which accounts for 8,196 denominations; (3) Orthodox, which accounts for 580 denominations; (4) Non-White Indigenous, which accounts for 10,956 denominations; (5) Anglican, which accounts for 240 denominations; (6) Marginal Protestant, which includes Jehovah's Witnesses, Mormons, New Age groups, and all cults,[7] and which accounts for 1,490 denominations; and (7) Catholic (Non-Roman), which accounts for 504 denominations.

According to Barrett's calculations, there are 8,196 denominations within Protestantism—not 25,000 as Roman Catholic apologists so cavalierly and carelessly claim. Barrett is also quick to point out that one cannot simply assume that this number will continue to grow each year; hence, the typical Roman Catholic projection of an annual increase in this number is simply not a given. Yet even this figure is misleading; for it is clear that Barrett defines "distinct denominations" as any group that might have a slightly different emphasis than another group (such as the difference between a Baptist church that emphasizes hymns, and a another Baptist church that emphasizes praise music).

No doubt the same Roman Catholic apologists who so gleeful-ly cite the erroneous 25,000-denominations figure, and who might with just as much glee cite the revised 8,196-denominations figure, would reel at the notion that there might actually be 223 distinct denominations within Roman Catholicism! Yet that is precisely the number that Barrett cites for Roman Catholicism.

Moreover, Barrett indicates in the case of Roman Catholicism that even this number can be broken down further to produce 2,942 separate "denominations"—and that was only in 1970! In that same year there were only 3,294 Protestant denominations; a difference of only 352 denominations. If we were to use the Roman Catholic apologist's method to "project" a figure for the current day, we could no doubt postulate a number upwards of 8,000 Roman Catholic denominations today! Hence, if Roman Catholic apologists want to argue that Protestantism is splintered into 8,196 "bickering" denom-inations, then they must just as readily admit that their own ecclesial system is splintered into at least 2,942 bickering denominations (possibly as many as 8,000). If, on the other hand, they would rath-er claim that among those 2,942+ (perhaps 8,000?) Roman Catho-lic denominations there is "unity," then they can have no objection to the notion that among the 8,196 Protestant denominations there is also unity.

In reality, Barrett indicates that what he means by "denomina-tion" is any ecclesial body that retains a "jurisdiction" (i.e., semi-autonomy). As an example, Baptist denominations comprise approx-imately 321 of the total Protestant figure. Yet the lion's share of Baptist denominations are independent, making them (in Barrett's calculation) separate denominations. In other words, if there are ten

Independent Baptist churches in a given city, even though all of
them are identical in belief and practice, each one is counted as a
separate denomination due to its autonomy in jurisdiction. This
same principle applies to all independent or semi-independent
denominations. And even beyond this, all Independent Baptist
denominations are counted separately from all *other* Baptist denominations, even though there might not be a dime's worth of difference among them. The same principle is operative in Barrett's count
of Roman Catholic denominations. He cites 194 Latin-rite denominations in 1970, by which Barrett means separate jurisdictions (or
diocese). Again, a distinction is made on the basis of jurisdiction,
rather than differing beliefs and practices.

However Barrett has defined "denomination," it is clear that he
does not think of these as major distinctions; for that is something he
reserves for another category. In addition to the seven major ecclesiastical "blocs" (mentioned above), Barrett breaks down each of
these traditions into smaller units that might have significant differences (what he calls "major ecclesiastical traditions," and what we
might normally call a *true* denomination).[8] Referring again to our
seven major ecclesiastical "blocs" (mentioned above, but this time in
reverse order): For (1) Catholic (Non-Roman), there are *four* traditions, including Catholic Apostolic, Reformed Catholic, Old Catholic, and Conservative Catholic; for (2) Marginal Protestants, there
are *six* traditions; for (3) Anglican, there are *six* traditions; for (4)
Non-White Indigenous, which encompasses third-world peoples
(among whom can be found traces of Christianity mixed with the
major tenets of their indigenous pagan religions), there are *twenty*
traditions, including a branch of Reformed Catholic and a branch of
Conservative Catholic; for (5) Orthodox, there are *nineteen* traditions; for (6) Protestant, there are *twenty-one* traditions; and for (7)
Roman Catholic, there are *sixteen* traditions, including Latin-rite local, Latin-rite catholic, Latin/Eastern-rite local, Latin/Eastern-rite
catholic, Syro-Malabarese, Ukrainian, Romanian, Maronite, Mel-
kite, Chaldean, Ruthenian, Hungarian, plural Oriental rites, Syro-
Malankarese, Slovak, and Coptic. It is important to note here that
Barrett places these sixteen Roman Catholic traditions (i.e., *true*

denominations) on the very same level as the twenty-one Protestant traditions (i.e., *true* denominations). In other words, the true count of real denominations within Protestantism is twenty-one, whereas the true count of real denominations within Roman Catholic is sixteen. Combined with the other major ecclesiastical blocs, that puts the total number of actual denominations in the world at ninety-two[9]—obviously nowhere near the 23,000 or 25,000 figure that Roman Catholic apologists constantly assert—and that figure of ninety-two denominations *includes* the sixteen denominations of Roman Catholicism!

As we have shown, the larger figures mentioned earlier (8,196 Protestant denominations and perhaps as many as 8,000 Roman Catholic denominations) are based on jurisdiction rather than differing beliefs and practice. Obviously, neither of those figures represents a true denominational distinction. Hence, Barrett's broader category (which we have labeled *true* denominations) of twenty-one Protestant denominations and sixteen Roman Catholic denominations represents a much more realistic calculation.

Moreover, Barrett later compares Roman Catholicism to Evangelicalism, which is a considerably smaller subset of Protestantism (so far as the number of denominations is concerned), and which is really the true category for those who hold to *sola Scriptura*.[10] Any comparison that the Roman Catholic apologist would like to make between *sola Scriptura* as the guiding principle of authority, and Rome as the guiding principle of authority (which we have demonstrated earlier is a false comparison in any case), needs to compare *true sola Scriptura* churches (i.e., Evangelicals) to Rome, rather than all Protestant churches to Rome. An Evangelical, as defined by Barrett, is someone who is characterized by (1) a personal conversion experience, (2) a reliance upon the Bible as the sole basis for faith and living, (3) an emphasis on evangelism, and (4) a conservative theology.[11] Interestingly, when discussing Evangelicals Barrett provides no breakdown, but rather treats them as one homogeneous group. However, when he addresses Roman Catholics on the very same page, he breaks them down into four major groups: (1) Catholic Pentecostals (Roman Catholics involved in the organized

Catholic Charismatic Renewal); (2) Christo-Pagans (Latin American Roman Catholics who combine folk-Catholicism with traditional Amerindian paganism); (3) Evangelical Catholics (Roman Catholics who also regard themselves as Evangelicals); and (4) Spiritist Catholics (Roman Catholics who are active in organized high or low spiritism, including syncretistic spirit-possession cults). And of course, we all know that this list can be supplemented by distinctions between moderate Roman Catholics (represented by almost all Roman Catholic scholars), Conservative Roman Catholics (represented by Scott Hahn and most Roman Catholic apologists), Traditionalist Roman Catholics (represented by apologist Gerry Matatics), and Sedevacantist Roman Catholics (those who believe the chair of Peter is currently vacant).

In any case, once we inquire into the source of the infamous "25,000-Protestant-denominations" figure one point becomes crystal clear. Whenever and at whatever point Barrett compares *true* denominations and differences among either Protestants or Evangelicals to those of Roman Catholicism, Roman Catholicism emerges almost as splintered as Protestantism, and even more splintered than Evangelicalism. That levels the playing field significantly. Whatever charge of "doctrinal chaos" Roman Catholic apologists wish to level against Protestantism may be leveled with equal force—and perhaps even greater force—against the doctrinal chaos of Roman Catholicism. Obviously, the Roman Catholic apologist can take little comfort in the fact that he has only sixteen denominations while Protestantism has twenty-one; and he can take even less comfort in the fact that while Evangelicalism has *no* divisional breakdown, Roman Catholicism has at least four major divisions.

If the Roman Catholic apologist wants instead to cite 8,196 idiosyncrasies within Protestantism, then he must be willing to compare that figure to at least 2,942 (perhaps upwards of 8,000 these days) idiosyncrasies within Roman Catholicism. In any case, he *cannot* compare the one ecclesial tradition of Roman Catholicism to 25,000, 8,196, or even twenty-one Protestant denominations; for Barrett places Roman Catholicism (as a single ecclesial tradition) on the same level as Protestantism (as a single ecclesial tradition).

In short, Roman Catholic apologists have hurriedly, carelessly—and, as a result, irresponsibly—glanced at Barrett's work, found a large number (22,189), and arrived at all sorts of absurdities that Barrett never concluded. One can only hope that, upon reading this critique, Roman Catholic apologists will finally put this argument to bed. The more likely scenario, however, is that the death of this argument will come about only when Evangelicals consistently point out this error—and correct it—each time it is raised by a Roman Catholic apologist. Sooner or later they will grow weary of the embarrassment that accompanies citing erroneous figures in a public forum.

Conclusion: Rome's Infallible Interpreter and the Land of Misfit Toys

MOST READERS of this book are no doubt familiar with the animated Christmas story, *Rudolf the Red-nosed Reindeer*, that airs virtually nonstop during the Christmas season. In that story, Rudolf and his associates visit the Land of Misfit Toys, a land filled with unwanted toys; unwanted because they either don't work at all, or they do something other than that which their names imply. Rome's infallible interpreter falls into this category as well. The Roman church is littered with private, individual interpretations of both Scripture *and* official church teachings; and her infallible interpreter (namely, the pope) has proven to be functionally useless. In the spirit of misfit toys, he is an infallible interpreter who doesn't infallibly interpret.

What are the ramifications of all we have discussed? First and foremost, we have for too long now allowed the Roman Catholic apologist to get away with impaling us on the horns of a false dilemma. The "How do you know" argument posed by the Roman Catholic apologist is a pet argument to be sure, but one to which we should no longer succumb.

1. When the Roman Catholic apologist asks, "How do you know your private interpretation of the Bible is correct over against the private interpretation of every other denomination?," we should respond by asking a question of our own: "How do you know that your private interpretation of Roman documents is correct over against the private interpretation of other Roman Catholics?

2. When the Roman Catholic apologists asks, "How can you be certain that you are in the truth since all you have to go on is your own fallible private judgment that your church is right?," we should counter with a similar question: "How can you be certain that you are in the truth since all you have to go on is your own fallible private judgment that Rome is right?"

3. When the Roman Catholic apologist asks, "How do you know you've picked the right denomination?," we should respond by asking, "How do you know you've picked the right infallible interpreter?"

4. When the Roman Catholic apologist insists that the principle of *sola Scriptura* has resulted in over 25,000 denominations, we should in turn insist that the principle of Scripture plus an infallible interpreter has resulted in an even greater number of religious cults.

The validity and strength of the principle of *sola Scriptura* is best illustrated in this comparison. If we all—Protestant, Roman Catholic, and Eastern Orthodox alike; all of us—were to use the principle of *sola Scriptura*, we would, with few exceptions, arrive at near unanimity about what the Bible teaches; and as a result, would embrace each other as brothers in Christ. In other words, contrary to the claims of Roman Catholic apologists, *sola Scriptura* results in *a relatively unified system of belief.* However, if all of us, instead, were to use the "infallible interpreter" principle, which excludes private judgment as legitimate (although, as we have seen, even those who claim this end up using it to decide among competing infallible interpreters), then we would invariably end up in mutually contradictory and mutually condemning religious systems.

This is not a mere hypothetical—this is, in fact, what the current state of affairs is. All those who embrace the "infallible interpreter" principle (Roman Catholics, Eastern Orthodox, Mormons, Jehovah's Witnesses, etc.) are demonstrably much more *disunified* than are all those who embrace the principle of *sola Scriptura*. In other words, if we do away with *sola Scriptura* and embrace the "infallible interpreter" principle, the result is nothing but uncertain chaos and tens of thousands of mutually contradictory religious groups. If, on the other hand, we do away with all infallible interpreters and embrace the principle of *sola Scriptura*, we get near unanimity in all essential areas of belief. Cast in this light, the pet argument of the Roman Catholic apologist—namely, that *sola Scriptura* results in doctrinal anarchy—is turned on its head. It is rather the case that the Roman Catholic apologist's *own* rule of faith—namely, Scripture plus an infallible interpreter—is the real cause of doctrinal anarchy. The antidote for this doctrinal anarchy is not to unify under a supposed infallible interpreter; there is no such animal, and even if there were we could never know for certain which one of the tens of thousands of candidates is the right one. The antidote instead lies in a return to Scripture alone, which, no matter how many denominations it may produce, unites those denominations in the essentials of the Evangelical faith. This is a much truer picture of biblical unity than the Roman Catholic alternative could ever hope for.

The primary Roman Catholic objection to *sola Scriptura*, namely that it is a "self-refuting proposition," is *itself* a self-refuting proposition. In order for any honest-minded Roman Catholic to arrive at the conclusion that Rome is the true church which alone can rightly understand and interpret the Scriptures for us, that Roman Catholic must first *privately* interpret that very same data for himself. Yet the instant that Roman Catholic does this, he has tacitly admitted that one *can* understand the Scriptures and church history *without* the help of the Roman Catholic church.

Appendix A: Real Life Encounters

ONE OF THE best ways to learn how to answer Roman Catholic claims is to see it modeled. Below I have included a sampling of how an Evangelical apologist might handle various Roman Catholic claims to authority, or Roman Catholic objections to *sola Scriptura*. I have purposefully kept the number of samples to a minimum. The number of possible note-worthy samples is virtually endless, and we would never be able to include them all in this little book. Hopefully, those I have included, along with the other information found in this book, will be enough to demonstrate the profound weakness of the Roman Catholic position on this issue, and to get you thinking in the right direction. Both the Roman Catholic statements, as well as their corresponding Evangelical responses are actual dialogues that have taken place in various forums. Only slight editing has been done for the sake of clarification.

Roman Catholic Statement #1: "Of course, you are only another fallible interpreter of scripture just like the rest of us, and your interpretation of these passages carries little weight."

Evangelical Response (Contribution by Jason Engwer): As though the words of Scripture don't have any objective meaning? If a passage says, "Jesus wept," would you actually suggest that the interpretation "James laughed" is just as valid as the interpretation "Jesus shed tears"? After all, both interpreters are fallible, so each of their interpretations must be just as valid as the other, right? Obviously, saying that we can't rely on a hierarchy in Rome to "infallibly" interpret the Scriptures for us is not equivalent to saying that Scripture is wholly subjective and open to any interpretation. To suggest that we can't have any grasp on Scripture unless some entity like the Roman Catholic Church interprets it for us is absurd. As I keep emphasizing, the Catholic position on this issue defeats itself. The material that would identify the "infallible interpreter" for you is the material that you supposedly can't understand without the "infallible interpreter." What if the Roman Catholic Church isn't actually the "infallible interpreter"? What if it's actually the Old Catholic Church? Or Eastern Orthodoxy? Or Mormonism? If you would let the Mormon church interpret the Scriptures for you, perhaps you would discover that the Mormon church has the authority to interpret Scripture for you. Wouldn't you be skeptical if the Mormon church claimed that it must interpret the Scriptures for you, and then dismissed anybody who disagrees on the basis that they only disagree because they're relying on their own "personal interpretation"?

Roman Catholic Statement #2: "I am studying the Bible and after checking into several different churches I have just about made up my mind on which Church is the church founded by Jesus Christ who is still very much working within the church and protects its doctrines and dogmas. I have run out of reasons to not join this Church. I would like someone to give me one reason why I should not join the Holy Roman Catholic Church."

Evangelical Response: Perhaps you have been fooled into believing the "canon" argument posited by Roman Catholic apologists; namely, that unless we ascribe authority and infallibility to the Roman Catholic church, we can have no assurance of the contents of the New Testament canon. But did you know that the same synods that Roman Catholic apologists point to for the list of New Testament books (Hippo and Carthage) also provide a list of Old Testament books that differs from the current Old Testament canon of the Roman Catholic church? Did you know that the Eastern church beat Rome to the correct list by some 20 years, and that Rome had omitted the book of Hebrews but eventually decided to adopt the list from the Eastern church? And by the way, on what basis are you entering the Roman Catholic church and rejecting the Eastern Orthodox church as the "true" church if your criteria is some kind of apostolic succession and ecclesial pedigree? If you say that your reason is the supposed Petrine Primacy found in Matthew 16, then you are arguing in a circle. For you have interpreted this Scripture as an individual and rendered a private judgment that Rome is right in her interpretation—but this is the very thing that Rome tells you is an illegitimate practice to begin with. One finds passages in the New Testament that seem to contradict Roman belief, and Rome invariably says that you as an individual are incapable of interpreting the Scriptures apart from Rome. And so the very principle that you say led you to Rome ends up being an illegitimate principle once you get to Rome. Ironic, isn't it? Moreover, Eastern Orthodoxy, which also claims to be the "true" church and which boasts direct apostolic succession, believes that you are misinterpreting the "Petrine Primacy" passages, and also claims that you cannot rightly interpret the Scriptures or church history apart from the Eastern Orthodox church. So now on what basis do you decide which "true" church is the *true* "true" church? Again, the irony of such a question demonstrates the utter silliness of joining either one of these "true" churches. Both have shied away from a strictly biblical examination (since both would utterly fail), claiming instead that one must search for the "true" church in the annals of history. Yet both have the same credentials of "pedigree, tradition, and liturgy"; and both deny that you are capable of rightly understanding history or the Scriptures without them. So, in order to pick one, you must engage in the very practice that both of them condemn as illegitimate. Yet you cannot pick both of them, for they see each other as illegitimate. So again, you are left in a dilemma. You either use the "illegitimate" principle of *sola Scriptura* and private judgment to decide which one is the "true" church; or you decide that the principle of *sola Scriptura* and private judgment is not so illegitimate after all, in which case you remain within Evangelicalism and reject Roman Catholicism and Eastern Orthodoxy. There is no other option.

Roman Catholic Statement #3: "I converted to Catholicism from Evangelicalism for this reason: *sola Scriptura* is kind of like a merry-go-round loop where it is impossible to prove anything since it is up to the reader to be the interpreter. See where I am going? Back to where I started if Scripture alone is my guide! Then, nobody can prove anything, and the merry-go-round spins again."

Evangelical Response: It's not quite that simple. To make the journey from the Evangelical church to the Catholic church, you must have followed one of at least two routes: (A) You gave up on any hope of figuring out the Bible for yourself, and decided to take a blind, existential leap into the arms of Rome, hoping you made the right choice (I'll give you more credit than to have followed this path, but it is an option); or (B) you looked at the Scriptures and the fathers and you discovered in them an infallible magisterium, unbroken apostolic succession, and all the other distinctively Roman tenets. If you chose (B), then you are in a dilemma. Rome teaches that one cannot trust his own private interpretation of Scripture or the fathers without the help and guidance of Rome. The reason for this is that the Scriptures are not formally sufficient (i.e., we also need unwritten tradition and Rome's interpretation to understand them correctly). Now, either Rome interpreted these things for you along the way, and you just accepted her interpretation (in which case you belong in category [A] above), or you interpreted the Scriptures and the Fathers on your own (without the help of Rome), in which case (according to Rome) you may very well be wrong in your conclusion. If you fall into this latter category, then could you please tell us, How can you be certain that your interpretation of the Scriptures and the fathers is correct in that they point to Rome, when so many others of us have read those same Scriptures and those same fathers and have come to completely different conclusions about them? Aren't you doing the very think Rome says you cannot do; namely, trusting your own private interpretation of the Scriptures and the fathers? There are obviously many other options from which to choose when one has chosen to abandon *sola Scriptura* in favor of an "infallible" magisterium. Why didn't you choose Eastern Orthodoxy who makes similar claims to the Scriptures and the fathers as does Rome? Why not choose Mormonism, whose "infallible magisterium" in Utah claims that the great apostasy predicted by

Paul took place in the immediate centuries following the apostles (note that they, too, have an explanation of Scripture and the fathers)? They also claim that you cannot understand the Scriptures properly without their help, and that both Scripture and church history must be interpreted in light of the *Book of Mormon, Doctrine and Covenants,* and the *Pearl of Great Price.* Why didn't you choose the Watchtower Society (the "infallible magisterium" of the Jehovah's Witnesses) who likewise says you cannot understand Scripture on your own, and that a proper interpretation can be had only by submitting to the Watchtower Society? Likewise with the Seventh-Day Adventists, whose "infallible interpreter" is Ellen G. White? Likewise with the Way International whose "infallible" founder's interpretation you need before you can understand the Scriptures correctly? The bottom-line question is: On what basis did you happen to choose *Rome* over these other options? *That* you cannot answer without engaging in the very practice that you insist makes the merry-go-round spin; namely, private interpretation.

Appendix B: The Roman Catholic Teaching on Private Interpretation

I INCLUDE this section because there are many Roman Catholics who deny that they argue in the way this book represents. When confronted with these epistemological fallacies, rather than present a defense of the Roman Catholic view, they claim that the fallacies are meaningless since Rome has never condemned private interpretation in the way this book suggests. I have included writings from Trent, Vatican I and Vatican II, to demonstrate the contrary; namely, that Rome really does condemn private interpretation, and that individual Roman Catholics really do commit the epistemological fallacies we have enumerated. I have italicized text within each council's documents to draw attention to the relevant points. Where clarification of a point is necessary, I have interspersed my own comments, offset in bracketed italicized text.

Vatican I Council

"Likewise I [the Bishop of Rome] accept sacred scripture *according to that sense which holy mother church held and holds, since it is her right to judge of the true sense and interpretation of the holy scriptures*; nor will I ever receive and interpret them except according to the unanimous consent of the fathers" (Session II, 3).

"Everybody knows that those heresies, condemned by the fathers of Trent, which rejected the divine magisterium of the church and *allowed religious questions to be a matter for the judgment of each individual*, have gradually collapsed into a multiplicity of sects, either at variance or in agreement with one another; and by this means a good many people have had all faith in Christ destroyed" (Session III, 5).

The Council of Trent

"Furthermore, in order to restrain petulant spirits, It decrees, that *no one, relying on his own skill*, shall,—in matters of faith, and of morals pertaining to the edification of Christian doctrine,—wresting the sacred Scripture to his own senses, *presume to interpret the said sacred Scripture contrary to that sense which holy mother Church, —whose it is to judge of the true sense and interpretation of the holy Scriptures,*—has held and does hold, or even contrary to the unani mous consent of the Fathers; even though such interpretations were never (intended) to be at any time published. Contraveners shall be made known by their Ordinaries, and be punished with the penalties by law established" (Session IV, "Decree Concerning the Edition, and the Use, of the Sacred Books").

Vatican II Council

"But *the task of authentically interpreting the Word of God*, whether written or handed on, *has been entrusted exclusively to the living teaching office of the Church.*... It is clear, therefore, that sacred tradition, sacred Scripture and the teaching authority of the Church, in accord with God's most wise design, are so linked and joined together that one cannot stand without the others, and that all together and each in its own way under the action of the one Holy Spirit contribute effectively to the salvation of souls." ("Dogmatic Constitution On Divine Revelation" [*Dei Verbum*] II, 10).

[The council goes on to assert a contradictory principle]:

"To search out the intention of the sacred writers, attention should be given, among other things, to 'literary norms.' For truth is set forth and expressed differently in texts which are variously historical, prophetic, poetic, or of other forms of discourse. The interpreter must investigate what meaning the sacred writer intended to express and actually expressed in particular circumstances by using contemporary literary forms in accordance with the situation of his own time and culture. *For the correct understanding of what the sacred author wanted to assert, due attention must be paid to the customary and characteristic styles of feeling, speaking and narrating which prevailed at the time of the sacred writer, and to the patterns men normally employed at the period in their everyday dealings with one another."* (Ibid., III, 12 ["Sacred Scripture, Its Inspiration and Divine Interpretation"]).

[The principle is contradictory, because those who follow it will invariably depart from the Roman Catholic interpretations on many issues, including Mary's perpetual virginity, Mary's status among the NT writers, Mary's role as mediator, as well as a host of other issues. Predictably, the council is quick to revert back to its original position in the very same section]:

"For *all of what has been said about the way of interpreting Scripture is subject finally to the judgement of the Church,* which carries out the divine commission and ministry of guarding and *interpreting the Word of God"* (Ibid.).

[The council likewise addresses the study and interpretation of the patristic writers as it pertains to private interpretation]:

"The bride of the Incarnate Word, the Church taught by the Holy Spirit, is concerned to move ahead toward a deeper understanding of the sacred Scriptures so that she may increasingly feed her sons with the divine words. Therefore, she also encourages the study of the holy Fathers of both East and West and of the sacred liturgies. Catholic exegetes then and other students of sacred theology, working diligently together and using appropriate means, should devote their energies, *under the watchful care of the sacred teaching office of the Church,* to an exploration and exposition of the divine writings" (Ibid., VI, 23 ["Sacred Scripture in the Life of the Church"]).

[Contrary to the claims of some modern Roman Catholic apologists, the Roman Catholic church does indeed condemn private interpretation of both the Scriptures and the writings of the church fathers. "Private interpretation" is defined in these documents as any interpretation that is contrary to what the Roman Catholic church has decided the meaning is. Obviously, any religious system could claim that—and many in fact have. Therefore, individual Roman Catholics do indeed commit the epistemological fallacies presented in this book; for in evaluating the claims of Rome, each and every one of them must interpret the Scriptures and church history for themselves to decide that it is Rome who is the true guardian of the truth, and not some other contender.]

Notes

1. *Dei Verbum*, Chapter III, *Sacred Scripture, Its Inspiration And Divine Interpretation*, 1.1, 4-5.

2. See Eric Svendsen, *Evangelical Answers: A Critique of Current Roman Catholic Apologists* (New York: Reformation Press, 1999), 119-152.

3. See for instance any bio of Roman Catholic apologist Gerry Matatics, in which he claims to have been a "Protestant theologian" before his conversion to Rome. Similar claims of grandeur are hinted at by other Protestants-turned-Catholic, including Scott Hahn and others. The intent of these claims is to demonstrate that if even leading, well-informed Protestants are converting to Rome, perhaps you should too. However, if these men were really leading Protestants, one wonders why the rest of us had never heard of them before their conversions.

4. Ed. David A. Barrett; New York: Oxford University Press, 1982.

5. Ibid., 17.

6. Ibid., 14-15.

7. Ibid., 14. While Barrett labels these groups as "Marginal *Protestants*," he makes it clear that they are much more reminiscent of Roman Catholicism in kind since they subscribe to a supplemental source of revelation outside of the Bible (57-58; see also 71).

8. Ibid., 14.

9. Ibid., 15. Barrett goes on to note that this figure includes all denominations with a membership of over 100,000. There are an additional sixty-four denominations worldwide, distributed among the seven major ecclesiastical blocs.

10. Most Protestant denominations today, being liberal denominations (thereby dismissing the authority of the Bible), do not hold to *sola Scriptura*, except perhaps as a formality.

11. Barrett, 71.

Resources for Epologists

On the dedication page of this book I made mention of "*e*-pologists." In case the reader is wondering just what that is, "*e*-pologist" (or, simply, "epologist") is a nomenclature that I have coined for those who do apologetics primarily, or exclusively, over the Internet. What follows is a list of Internet resources for Evangelical epologists, whether they are amateur- or lay-apologists. The list is not exhaustive; only helpful in providing direction to those looking for answers and counter-arguments in defense of those who seek to destroy the Faith.

New Testament Research Ministries
> http://www.ntrmin.org; the web site of my ministry

Alpha and Omega Ministries
> http://www.aomin.org; the web site of James White

Christian Resources
> http://www.christiantruth.com; the web site of William Webster

Christian Liberty
> http://members.aol.com/jasonte; the web site of Jason Engwer

Grace Unknown
> http://www.graceunknown.com; the web site of Tim Enloe

Theologically Correct dot com Ministries
> http://theologicallycorrect.com; the web site of Kerry Gilliard

The Strait Gate
> http://www.straitgate.com; the web site of Steven Luker; full of Reformed resources and RealAudio debates, teaching sermons and lectures

Gospel Outreach
> http://www.gospeloutreach.net; the web site of Rolaant L. McKenzie

CARM
> http://www.carm.org; CARM stands for Christian Apologetics and Research Ministry, and is the web site of Matthew Slick

The Bible Gateway
> http://bible.gospelcom.net; searchable Bible versions and foreign-language translations

Bible Study Tools
> http://www.biblestudytools.net; a compendium of online Bible study tools, including concordances, lexicons, commentaries, Bible dictionaries, interlinears, patristic writings, etc.

Early Church Fathers
> http://www.ccel.org/fathers2; a searchable database of patristic writings from Calvin College

The Perseus Project
> http://www.perseus.tufts.edu; an advanced tool from Tufts University that allows searches of ancient Greek and Latin writings; great for determining how New Testament words were used in the common literature of the day

Greek Language and Linguistic Gateway
> http://www.greek-language.com; much like the Perseus Project, but the focus is on ancient and Hellenistic Greek writings

About the Author

ERIC SVENDSEN holds a Master of Arts in New Testament studies from Trinity Evangelical Divinity School, a Doctorate in Theological Studies from Columbia Evangelical Seminary, and has recently completed his dissertation for a Ph.D. in New Testament from Greenwich School of Theology, U.K. He is the founder and director of New Testament Research Ministries, an apologetics ministry specializing in Roman Catholic/Evangelical dialogue. He has authored several books, including *Evangelical Answers: A Critique of Current Roman Catholic Apologists* (Lindenhurst, N.Y.: Reformation Press, 1999), *The Table of the Lord: An Examination of the Setting of the Lord's Supper in the New Testament and Its Significance as an Expression of Community* (New Testament Restoration Foundation, 1996), *Who Is My Mother? The Role and Status of the Mother of Jesus in the New Testament and Roman Catholicism* (Amityville, NY: Calvary Press, 2001), *Getting To Know Your Bible: A Two-Year Plan for Becoming a Bible Expert in Just 30 Minutes a Day!* (Denver: New Testament Research Ministries, 2001), and *Learning to Master Your Bible: A Guide to Plumbing the Depths of God's Word* (Denver: New Testament Research Ministries, 2001). Eric is active in engaging anti-Christians in public debate, and has appeared as a guest on numerous Christian radio talk shows, including CRI's "The Bible Answer Man" broadcast. You may contact Eric Svendsen through his ministry's web site at www.ntrmin.org.